Where is the Meat?

A Bible Study of Book of Genesis

The Beginning

By Hannah H. O' Dunnahey

Introduction

I find that when I am doing a Bible study with a group of people they pick a Bible study that does not really fill me spiritually. So, I am writing my own Bible study that has more "Bible meat" in it for those of us who are starving for more but not getting it from the "Bible milk" studies. I will go through the Bible, book by book and subject by subject to get to the "meatier" parts of the Bible. Not only do I want to use the Bible but other references so we can see the whole picture.

With the book of Genesis, I not only go in more depth of what the Bible says but also talk about the theories and science that tries to disprove the Bible. I show that science actually shows that the Bible is true and accurate. Since the book of Genesis covers many of the lives of the Patriarchs of the foundation of several religions; I will cut it down to cover more of each of these lives.

I wrote this Bible study the way that I study my personal Bible study. I ask questions to help me figure out what the text is really saying. This helps me personally with diving deeper into my understanding. The Hand Outs are what I discovered and my understanding of the research to help me see the bigger picture of human understanding.

Table of Contents

Hand Out

Genesis Chapter 1

In the Beginning

The first five books of the Bible are sometimes called the Pentateuch which means "five books." They are also known as the books of the law because they contain the laws and instructions given by the Lord through Moses to the people of Israel. These books were written by Moses; except for the last portion of Deuteronomy because it tells about the death of Moses. These five books lay the foundation for the coming of Christ in that here God chooses and brings into being the nation of Israel. As God's chosen people, Israel became the custodians of the Old Testament, the recipients of the covenants of promise, and the channel of Messiah (Rom. 3:2; 9:1-5). Genesis is a Greek word that means, Beginning. The book of Genesis is the first book listed in the bible; however, it is not the first book written. Job is considered the oldest book written in the Old Testament. Bible scholars say it was written during the time of Abraham. They are not sure who the author is.

If we cannot believe what the Bible says in Genesis then how can we believe what it says anywhere else?

Genesis 1:1 In the beginning God created the heaven and the earth.

What do we see in the very first sentence of Genesis? We see that God created.

Who is this God?

We now call this entity God the Father. For many generations He has been called Yeh ô v â h (pronounced as yeh-ho-vaw.) It means the self-existent or eternal.

Genesis 1:1-2 Is there a controversy of two Earths between verse one and verse two?

When people read verse one and verse two, they see two different Earths. However, that is not what I see. I see an introductory sentence then the author going into more detail from that introduction. The same thing happens when we get to Adam and Eve. We are told when God made them male and female at the end of Chapter one. Then the author goes into further detail of how God made them male and female in Chapter two.

The confusion of the two different Earths comes from the word void in verse two. If God created it in verse one then how can it be void by verse two? To answer this question let's examine the word void. Void here simply means to be empty. There was nothing here on earth; it was a floating chunk of rock and water.

Genesis 1:2 And the earth was without form, and void; and darkness was upon the face of the deep. And the Spirit of God moved upon the face of the waters.

What is another name for the Spirit of God? Holy Ghost.

What does the scripture mean when it says the Spirit of God moved upon the waters?

"Moved upon the waters," is similar in meaning as a hen brooding over an egg. She protects her egg, keeps it warm, and she does it with care so as not to break the egg. So, the Spirit of God also brooded over the Earth keeping it safe with love and care.

Genesis 1:3 And God said, Let there be light: and there was light.

What is the light source in this verse?

We do not see the creation of the sun until Genesis 1:16. So what is causing the light? There are Bible scholars who believe that the light source is Jesus himself. They get this idea from **John 8:12 Then spake Jesus again unto them, saying, I am the light of the world: he that followeth me shall not walk in darkness, but shall have the light of life.** We obviously do not know for certain what this light source is but it would be wonderful if it was Jesus himself shining His light upon the world.

If the light source was Jesus, then we would see the Holy Trinity in the first three lines of the Bible. God the Father who created the heaven and the earth. The Holy Spirit moved upon the water like a brooding hen with love and care. Then God the Son who is the Light of the World.

Critics will say that the Holy Trinity is an old idea stolen from older cultures. However, since the Torah, aka Bible is the oldest oral tradition it is the other cultures that stole this idea from the Israelites. Let us remember that this book was not written until Moses wrote it. It was told from one generation to another. The parts that humans did not know before; God told His prophet Moses.

The God Particle

See Hand Out #3

The Big Bang Theory

See Hand Out #1

Genesis 1:4 How does God separate the Light from the Darkness?

The Light was so intense that there was no darkness, no shadow anywhere. So, God had to turn down the brightness of the Light to even create darkness.

Many cultures associate light and darkness with good and evil. God is the light and Satan is the dark. But we see from Genesis 1:4 that God allows darkness. Satan does not actually control it. We see light and darkness as equal forces. In reality, light overrules darkness every time. God always wins!

Why does God have darkness?

Because of us. He made us and He knows that we require darkness to rest our bodies and minds. He prepared everything perfectly for us here on Earth. We will see the love and care God takes for us again and again.

Here is something else to think about. Since the fall of Lucifer and the ⅓ of the angels. They can no longer live in the light of God's presence. He had to tone down the light for them also. Even though they had fallen from God's grace He still loves them and cares for them.

We need to take that as an example to apply this to our own lives. To love the ones who would like to see us destroyed Matthew 5:44.

Genesis 1:5 What is needed to qualify a day?

See Hand Out #2 Space and Time

Light and darkness, morning and evening. This is the beginning of time itself. A 24hour day is born. From this point forward mankind will use the light and darkness to "tell the time." The ancients use sundials to tell time during the day.

Genesis 1:5-8 What did God make on the second day of creation?

This is the first Heaven. According to the Bible there are three layers of heaven. The first layer of heaven is what we now call the sky. From the ground to Innerspace, aka ozone layer. The second layer of heaven is what we now call outer space. This is where God will later put the Sun, moon, and stars. It is a vast amount of space but it is there for us. To give us an understanding of how small we are compared to God. The third layer of heaven is from outer space to the Throne of God. That is where we go when God calls us home.

Psalms 19:1-7 is a beautiful psalm about the heavens please read this scripture.

Genesis 1:9-10 What is on the Earth?

Is there any mention of mountains, frozen tundra, or desert?

How about different types of land mass? Like how we see different continents today.

Geologists will agree that all of the land mass was once grouped together in Earth's ancient past. It would have been flat to small hills but no mountain ranges. There was no frozen tundra or desert since those climates are difficult for a human to live in. God created the land and sea to support us. We will discuss later what happened to the Earth to make it look like it is today.

There is great debate as to how old the Earth is. Is it 6,000 years old or 4.5million. The answer is they are both correct. Who can agree that God can do whatever He wants to do? Can God create a planet for His children that is fully developed and ready for life? Then can He start that planet spinning on its axis shortly before He creates that child? Of course, He can. So, the planet can be both. The inner core of the planet can be fully developed and appear 4.5 million years old and it can start turning on its axis shortly before man is created and be 6,000 years old. We are on God's time frame not ours.

Another angle of this debate is that the time frame that is used is incorrect. They are using a fallible test to determine the age of the earth. They use a test that is called radiometric dating. The dictionary defines radiometric dating as this- "any method of determining the age of earth materials or objects of organic origin based on measurement of either short-lived radioactive elements or the amount of a long-lived radioactive element plus its decay product." However, when this test is put to the test it is flawed. When Mount Saint Helens erupted in the 1980's they tested a newly formed rock that was formed during the eruption. Radiometric dating is supposed to be able to rate the stones rate of decay. Radiometric dating said the stone was 3.4 million years old but in reality, the stone was only 10 years old when they performed the test. Many studies have been performed on similar rocks throughout the world and all the studies have proven that Radiometric dating is flawed and not reliable.

Genesis 1:11-13 God finishes the third day doing what?

On the third day, God created the ozone layer, dry land, and vegetation. We can see that there are already herbs, fruit, and vegetables for all living things to eat. We have air to breathe, dry ground to stand on, and things to eat. Things that we take for granted with every breath, every step, and every meal. If it was not for God giving us these basic things, we would be completely different creatures.

Before we get into what God created next: I thought we would discuss creatures that people think are in Outer Space.

Please see Hand Out #4 What are Aliens?

Genesis 1:14-15 What did God just give us?

A calendar. For many generations humans have used the Sun, Moon and stars to tell the seasons of the year and predict future events. Many ancient human monuments are considered to track the movements in the heavens. Stonehenge in England, Pyramids of the Mayans in Central America, and many others all around the planet.

God put all those things in the sky for us to dream about, to imagine about, and to make us feel as small as we actually are. Each planet, moon, and star are put there for us to learn from, for us to realize how special we are in God's eyes.

Mercury is to teach us what we would look like if our planet was closer to the Sun. Venus is there to show us what a gas planet looks like closer to the Sun. Mars is to show us how important our ozone layer is to our survival. Jupiter is a protector, a gravity anchor, and just an awesome learning tool in so many ways. Saturn teaches us the beauty of gravitational rings. Uranus teaches us about a planet being on its side. Neptune teaches us about cold gasses. Even Pluto and other dwarf planets teach us something. Every Galaxy, every black hole, and every Nebula has something to teach us about how important and special we are to God.

Genesis 1:16 The bible calls the Sun and Moon what?

See Hand Out #5

God's Cosmic Time

See Hand Out #6

Genesis 1:17-19 Ends the fourth day.

We have a planet with water, solid ground, breathable air, and lush vegetation. We now have a Sun for warmth and light. We have the moon to show us the time, seasons, and to control the push and pull of the tides.

Genesis 1:20-23 Why is it important for the Moon to be created on the fourth day before the creatures that are created on the fifth day?

The Moon creates the tide of the oceans. That tide is needed to support the aquatic creatures on this planet. Without the tide there would be no oxygen in the water. Things would die without breathable oxygen in the water. When you have a planet with mostly water then you have living creatures in that water you have to give them an environment to support them. You see God loves all His creations, not just us.

Primordial Goo

See Hand Out #7

Genesis 1:24-25 What has God given us?

God has given us something to look after, to take care of, and things to take care of us. Most people do wish that God did not create those things that creep upon the earth. However, they are useful to us and our environments. We need beetles, spiders, and other crawly things.

Genesis 1:26 This is the verse most bible scholars will use to fight against Evolutionists. "Let us make man in our image." What does this statement truly mean to you?

Firstly, let's point out the fact that the words "us" and "our" are used.

Who are the "us" and "our?"

Right, God the Father, God the Son, and God the Holy Ghost.

Secondly, **what is meant by image in this verse? Does God have a human form? Are we all a physical likeness of God?** If so, **why do we all look so different from one another?**

God is spirit, which means that God the Father does not have a human body. God the Son came to earth in human form (John 1:1), but God the Father did not. Jesus is unique as Emmanuel, "God with us" (Matthew 1:23). Numbers 23:19 emphasizes God's truthfulness by contrasting Him with mortal men: "God is not human, that he should lie, not a human being, that he should change his mind."

Some question why the Bible sometimes speaks of God as if He has a body. For example, Isaiah 59:1 mentions God's "hand" and "ear." Second Chronicles 16:9 speaks of God's "eyes." Matthew 4:4 puts words in God's "mouth." In Deuteronomy 33:27 God has "arms." All of these verses are examples of anthropomorphism—a way of describing God with anatomical or emotional terms so that humans can better understand Him. The use of anthropomorphism, a form of figurative language, does not imply that God has an actual body.

To say that God is spirit is to say that God the Father is invisible. Colossians 1:15 calls God the "invisible God." First Timothy 1:17 praises God, saying, "To the King of the ages, immortal, invisible, the only God, be honor and glory forever and ever."

Even though God is spirit, He is also a living, personal being. As such, we can know Him personally. Joshua 3:10 speaks of God in this way, saying, "You will know that the living God is among you." Psalm 84:2 declares, "My heart and flesh sing for joy to the living God" (ESV).

Philosophically, God must be a spirit in order to be infinite. Also, if God was limited to a physical body, He could not be omnipresent (in all places at once). God the Father is not limited to the dimensional restrictions of created things but can exist in all places at one time. God is the uncreated First Cause that is the power behind all other beings.

Interestingly, in John 4:24 Jesus makes the connection between God being spirit and worshiping Him in spirit and in truth. The idea is that, since God is spirit, people must worship Him accurately (in truth) and in spirit (with their soul or heart), as opposed to relying on traditions, rituals, and physical locales.

We all look different because of Genetics. If you had Adam who is dark skin and Eve who is of a lighter complexion, they could create children with all kinds of different skin tones. Throughout time people can adapt to their environment. I want to point out that there are not different races of humans, just the human race. We are all part of the same family. We need to start treating one another that way.

Scientists who specialize in DNA (geneticist) have traced DNA codes of all humans back to one Father and one Mother pair. Again, scientists prove the bible true but are not willing to say so. They also have shown that the oldest strain of DNA code resides in Africa. Which could mean that one of Noah's sons went to Africa and settled there and did not stray very far from that spot.

This is where we come into some controversy and debate. There are some from Africa who will state that they are the true Jew and not the Israelite. Mostly because of the DNA code seeming to start there. I do not follow this line of thinking because of the fact that the bible is very clear as to who the Jewish people are. They are the sons of Abraham, Issaac, and Jacob. The tribe of Levites can still trace their family tree all the way back to Aaron, the first High Priest and to his brother, Moses. We know from the bible that Moses and Aaron's parents were from the tribe of Levites. So, to me, the Israelites are the true Jews.

There are what are called lost tribes of Israelites in Africa, mostly Ethiopia but other parts too. Queen Sheba was a wife to King Solomon and their son and her Heir was King of Ethiopia. There were other tribes in the history of Israel that fled to Africa during times of trouble.

Theory of Evolution

See Hand Out #8

Genesis 1:27 What has God created? Why does God create two different sexes?

If God had created us to be attracted to the same sex and we are born to be attracted to that sex then why create the opposite sex? Why not just Adam and Steve in the garden? Homosexuality goes against the very reason why there are two sexes. We are not born to be gay. We were created so that we can fill the Earth with our species. Adam and Steve would not be able to live on in their children. The human race would have died with them.

Yes, homosexuality is a sin. But it does not mean that we have to hate the sinner. If someone truly wanted to change from that lifestyle then God can do it. We cannot force someone to change. We can only show them a small sliver of God's love and love them no matter what. And pray.

Genesis 1:31 What is dominion?

According to the dictionary a definition of dominion is the **power or right of governing and controlling; sovereign authority.** The human race has the power and right to govern and control this planet. We definitely have abused that power over the years. But this world is ours to destroy or to protect.

God is the rightful owner of everything He creates but he has put us in charge of the Earth. We have the right to govern and control here on this planet. Have we given that power over to Satan over the years? Have we given away our dominion?

Genesis Chapter 2

Adam and Eve

Genesis 2:2-3 Why did God rest?

Why did God take a rest after He finished His work? Did he suddenly become tired? Did He run out of God juice? Jesus tells us that God rested for us. **Mark 2:27 Then he said to them, "The Sabbath was made for man, not man for the Sabbath.** We are the ones who need the rest, not God. We need to keep one day out of our busy lives to focus just on God and nothing else.

The Israelites kept the Sabbath from Friday evening when the Sun went down till Saturday night when the Sun went down. They did nothing that would be considered work during that time. However, you can take this no work thing to the extreme.

How did the Sabbath get moved from Saturday to Sunday?

See Hand Out #9

Is worshiping on Sunday a sin?

No, you are worshiping God, that could never be a sin. When and where you choose to worship God is between you and God. I would first pray and ask God what is right for you.

Genesis 2:6 How was the vegetation watered?

The vegetation is watered by dew. I want to point this out because it is an important point to the Noah Flood story. I will explain further when we get to Noah.

Genesis 2:7 Why is it important that God formed us from the dust of the ground?

God created this world where everything on it is made with a carbon atom in its substance. He made us be able to be compatible with this planet. We are a part of this world. This world is a part of us. We would struggle to live on another planet. We would struggle to live in space. We were created for this world and this world was created for us.

What is a living soul?

I have heard of a nurse who works in the field of fertilization. She is the person who takes the egg and the seed and puts them together. She has said that there is a spark if it goes right. If there is not a spark then she knows that the procedure did not work. The spark is life. Human life has a soul that belongs to God. What that life does with the soul is up to the life.

What is the breath of life?

The breath of life that God gives Adam, is what sets him apart from other creatures on this planet. Many studies have been performed on ape and human cognitive functions. One study was a simple problem-solving test. This test was performed on an adult ape and a 5-year-old human child. They gave both subjects a simple wood block and they simply viewed what both subjects would do with it. The ape stood the block up on one end. Because of the shape of the block, it would fall down. Ape stood it back up again and again it fell down. The 5year old child stood the block up. Just like the ape the block fell over. The child put it back on its end. The difference is the child tried to figure out why the block would not stay upright. The ape did not do this investigation. This understanding is the difference that God has given to human kind.

Genesis 2:8-14 Where is the Garden located?

The location of the ancient garden of Eden is lost to us. Many use these verses to try and locate the garden. The garden east of Eden is no longer in existence. It was wiped out by the global flood. We are left to guess where its location was.

To see a map of the area please see Hand Out #10

Genesis 2:15 What was Man's first job?

He was to have dominion over the garden. To protect and to keep it strong and healthy.

Genesis 2:16-17 What is God's first command? Why should Adam and Eve not have knowledge of good and evil?

Even though Adam and Eve were made as grown humans so they were capable of taking care of themselves. Their minds were empty like babies. A mind like that could not handle the complications of knowing sin. They needed to rely on the Father to tell them what was right and what was wrong.

Genesis 2:17 If Adam and Eve had not eaten of the tree of Knowledge would they have died at all?

Not only did eating of the fruit bring knowledge of sin but it also brought death. If they had not eaten off the tree, would humankind be immortal now? According to the scriptures we are to live with Jesus on this Earth for eternally after He has formed His Kingdom here on Earth. You did not need to die in order for you to be there. You could be the rare lucky few who survive the Tribulations to the very end and still live on forever with Jesus.

Genesis 2:18 What is a woman?

A woman is a helper. God created women to help others. Women are very good at their job. God knew exactly what man needed as a mate. That is why man is not as productive if he is single.

Genesis 2:19 What is man's second job?

Mankind is the only creature on this planet that is compelled to travel to the highest summits and to the deepest part of the seas. He definitely likes to name his discoveries. The only thing Christopher Columbus wanted from his travels was the ability to name what he found. By the way he was not the man who named the America's. But he did name the Indians, improperly.

Genesis 2:21-23 Why a rib?

All God really needed was a single cell from Adam. He could have taken a scraping from Adam's skin. He could have manipulated Adam's DNA to create a new sex. So, why a rib? This is to show that men and women are to work side by side. Women are not to be behind nor ahead of the man.

Genesis 2:24 Is this good marriage advice?

I will leave this question up to you to discuss.

Genesis Chapter 3

The Fall

Genesis 3:1-3 Who is the serpent?

Who is the Dragon in Revelation 13:4? Are these the same entity?

The Devil, aka Satan, aka our adversary starts as a small serpent and over time he becomes a powerful dragon ready to devour us. If you read the ending, you will find out we win. No matter how big and bad the adversary thinks he is. We still have the power to defeat him.

Genesis 3:4 Did the serpent lie to Eve?

Even though Adam and Eve did not die instantly when they bit into the forbidden fruit. However, death did enter the world because they did eat of the fruit.

Genesis 3:5 Does the Adversary tell us this lie still today?

We still see self-help books in bookstores. We still have religions telling people that they are gods. They don't need God; they can do it themselves. Those of us who believe in the Almighty God know that we can do nothing without Him.

Genesis 3:6 Was it really all Eve's fault that evil was now known to this world?

To be fair it was not all Eve's fault. Adam was capable of saying no to the fruit. God told Adam not to eat the fruit. Adam then told Eve not to eat the fruit. It was his responsibility to listen to God and not to his sinful wife. It was Adam's fault for not obeying God and for not correcting his wife. Instead, he joined her in her sin.

What kind of Fruit was on the tree?

If you said Apple then you are wrong. The apple comes from an artist rendering. According to Jewish tradition the fruit was a pomegranate.

Genesis 3:7 When did their eyes become open?

Their eyes did not become open to sin until they both ate from the fruit. So, if Adam did not also eat the fruit would their eyes become open? This is a question to ask God when we see Him.

Genesis 3:8-11 Was it God the Father who was in the garden?

I believe that it was actually Jesus who was walking in the garden. Jesus is the Word of God. Jesus was the one who formed everything. He is God's hands. Jesus has a physical form later in the Old Testament stories. We will cover that later.

Why did they hide?

They have been naked since the beginning of their creation. Why all of the sudden do they feel as though they need to hide their bodies? When they looked at each other after their eyes were open to sin. I think they really liked what they saw in each other's bodies. The sin of Lust over took them. What happens to male bodies when Lust takes over? This happened to Adam and he became ashamed of what his body was doing. So, he covered himself and made Eve cover herself. This is a logical theory that makes sense to me, not a biblical fact.

Genesis 3:12 What is Adam's response to God's question?

He does not acknowledge his part in the sin. He just blames everything on Eve. Man has blamed Eve for the world's sin since then.

Genesis 3:13 Who does Eve blame?

It was totally the serpent's fault to tempt Eve. Eve could also have said no to the fruit. But, she didn't.

Genesis 3:14 Is the serpent's punishment suitable for what he did?

The serpent, aka Satan, aka Devil, aka adversary was cursed above all beasts. His legs are taken away from him so he has to slither on the ground. All because he lied and tempted Eve into knowing sin.

There are fossils of snakes having legs at one time.

I also want to make a note that many religions throughout the ancient world and even present day use the snake as a symbol of their religion.

Genesis 3:15 Can this verse be applied to Jesus?

This is the very first biblical prophecy about the Messiah, aka Jesus. From this verse Satan knows that the Messiah will come from a virgin. He also knows that he will have an opportunity to harm the Messiah.

From this point forward the devil does what he can to deceive us about the Messiah. From the time of the tower of babel there has been a cult that uses the story of a virgin birth. Critics will use this information to claim that Christians stole the virgin birth from older religions. This is not the case. It is Satan who stole this idea from God.

Genesis 3:16 Did Eve have children while she was still in the garden?

It is a possibility that Eve did have children in the garden; otherwise, how would she know that giving birth was more painful. However, we do not read of her having any children until Cain and Abel.

Are men supposed to dominate women?

Men and women are still to be equal partners in life; however, men are meant to have the "final say" in how the family is ran. Paul tells us that men are to treat their wives like Christ treated the church. Christ sacrificed himself for the church. The key to a happy marriage is the trinity pyramid.

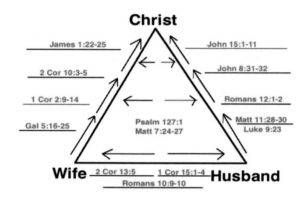

Genesis 3:17-19 What is cursed for the sake of Adam?

Later in the story of Adam and Eve this curse is better understood.

What just happened to all mankind?

While in the garden, God took care of Adam and Eve. As I have said before mentally, they were like children. They needed the Father to help them in all things. Now that evil was known in the world their mental capacity had grown with their knowledge. Now that man no longer needed God to lead them by the hand as a child. He treated them as though they were teenagers and kicked them out of the house to fend for themselves.

Their actions did not just affect Adam and Eve but all the generations that came after them. We could still be in the garden with our Father visiting us in the cool of the day. Now, we have to work for everything that we get.

Genesis 3:20 What does the name Eve mean?

In Hebrew the meaning of the name Eve is: Life, living. Adam means: a man. Eve was called woman until this point and now she has a name. Woman is the female version of man. Now that they are in trouble, they have names. Everyone knows that your full name is used when you are in trouble. This is probable where that tradition started from.

Genesis 3:21 Why is this verse important?

Please see Hand Out #11

Genesis 3:22-24 Why is Adam and Eve kicked out of the garden?

Most people will say that it is punishment for eating the forbidden fruit, but that is not the reason. God kicked Adam and Eve out of the garden to protect them and all of mankind.

What is the tree of life?

This tree was not forbidden to Adam and Eve before now. The tree of life gives a human the ability to live forever. This is why man needed to be protected from the tree from now on. Let's imagine an evil human, intent on doing harm to others, and they can live forever. All the villains who have lived throughout history would still be roaming the earth causing pain and sorrow to this day. This is why Adam and Eve needed to be separated from the tree of life.

Genesis Chapter 4

Murder comes to the Earth

Genesis 4:1 What does Cain's name mean?

Cain meaning "possessing" or "acquiring, to erect, to found," and "to create." Eve explicitly bases Cain's name upon the notion of acquiring: "Now Adam knew Eve, his wife, and she conceived and bore Cain, and said, "I have acquired a man from the Holy One." In order to farm or ranch Cain needs to "acquire" tools, animals, and the land itself. He is also the founder of a city.

Genesis 4:2 What does Abel's name mean?

Abel's name means "vapor" or "breath" – something that is here today and gone tomorrow. According to Proverbs, "The getting of treasures by a lying tongue is a fleeting vapor and a snare of death" (Prov 21:6).

Were Cain and Abel twins?

The Bible does not tell us that Cain and Abel are twins. An example is Esau and Jacob were twins.

Why is it important for us to know what Cain and Abel's jobs are?

Cain's job was to tend to the fields and Abel's job was to tend to the livestock. Why is it important that we know this? We see that the whole family is needed to support themselves now that God is no longer taking care of them. Even the children need to do manual labor to help support the entire family.

Genesis 4:3-6 Why is Cain's offering not accepted?

When sin entered into the world it contaminated the whole planet. Everything that grew was now tainted with sin. God could not accept a sinful offering. We see later in the book of Leviticus that God does eventually accept first fruits offerings but that is thousands of years in the future from this point. At this point in Bible history the ground is saturated with the first sin. Therefore, God cannot accept Cain's offering.

Genesis 4:7 What is God telling Cain?

If you're good then you are accepted. If you're bad then evil will overcome you and you can not fend him off.

Genesis 4:8 What sin is associated with this act?

Cain did not listen to God and evil overcame him. He became jealous of his brother and his relationship with God.

Genesis 4:9 This is the first what?

This is the first time a human has lied to God. God knew what happened between Cain and Abel, but like a good parent He wanted to see if the child would confess his sin.

Genesis 4:10 What does it mean that blood cries out?

Blood is the life force of the human body; it stores memories of that person. Those who have experienced a heart transplant say that they have developed certain characteristics from their donors. They have found that hearts carry memories and blood flows through them. God could hear the blood of Abel crying out seeking justice.

Genesis 4:11-13 What is Cain's punishment?

Cain is cursed again! He can no longer farm for food. He can still forge what is already grown from the ground, but he can no longer grow it himself.

We see from these scriptures that man was first farmers then nomads. Later we see that Cain builds a city. Within the first generation of man this all happens. Some scientists will say that man was nomads first, then farmers, then city dwellers. Man needed to learn how to create food for himself in preparation for his traveling. When people were moving "Out West" in the North America expansion they took supplies with them. That is the same thinking of the human race since Cain was forced to be nomadic.

Genesis 4:14-15 Why should other's kill Cain?

If others learn of Cain's sin and see his punishment, why would anyone want to put that on his own head? However, the human reaction to murder is vengeance we feel it is right to kill those who did the crime.

What is the mark of God a foreshadowing of?

Revelation 7:3 tells us that the servants of God will have a seal on their foreheads. This seal is to protect God's servants from what is to come. Just like the mark of God protects Cain from harm.

Genesis 4:17 Where did Cain get his wife?

Cain's wife was one of his sister's. It is interesting to note that there is a tradition outside the Scripture that can be proven in The Works of Josephus* which states that: "The number of Adam's children, as the old tradition says, was 33 sons and 23 daughters." Josephus is a Jewish Historical scholar who lived during the time of Jesus.

Genesis 4:23-24 What did one of Cain's descendants do?

Cain's descendant, Lamech, told his wives that he murdered two men.

Why did Lamech think he would be avenged by God if someone killed him?

Lamech killed two men because they attacked him first. So, he felt justified to kill them. If these men's loved ones wanted to take vengeance for their murder, then Lamech felt that God would seek justice on his behalf.

Genesis 4:25 What does Adam's third son's name mean?

Seth's name means appointed, placed.

Genesis 4:26 What does Enos mean?

Enos means mankind, mortal

Hand Out #1
The Big Bang Theory

Before we get too far into this debate let us define science. In its original form *science* simply meant "knowledge." Now, the denial of supernatural events limits the depth of understanding that science can have and the types of questions science can ask. Although naturalistic science claims to be neutral and unbiased, it starts with this bias. Making a distinction between operational (observational) science and historical (origins) science helps us to understand the limitations of these naturalistic presuppositions in science.

There are two different views about the beginning of creation. The big bang theory and the version in the bible. I will confess that I am no great scholar in either version but I will do my best to break them down so we can make sense out of it.

The Big Bang theory is the secular science version of trying to explain how the universe was formed. This version has a lot of holes in its theory, but the world is willing to accept it as fact because it does not have a God. Ironically, the one thing the big bang does not explain is the origin of the universe. It is only a story about what supposedly happened afterwards.

The naturalistic story of the solar system goes back 4.5 billion years. In this view the solar system began as a cloud of dust and gas that collapsed on itself. A star began to form as the cloud was compressed by some unknown force. As the star spun and collected more mass, a disk of dust began to form the planets. Over millions of years the young solar system was formed. Much debris was left over from the process and is present today as asteroids and large belts and clouds of material. There was no intervention by a Creator, as the physical laws of the universe are adequate to explain everything.

According to the secular scenario, energy was gradually converted into matter as the universe continued to expand after the big bang. That matter accumulated and the first atoms began to form. The first stages of the naturalistic universe contained only energy. As the expanding universe slowed and cooled, hydrogen, helium, and small amounts of lithium were formed from the energy. The gasses gathered into nebulae which then gave birth to stars and planets. As the earliest stars produced their energy through nuclear fusion, heavier elements were assembled and were eventually scattered into the universe as the stars exploded. These heavier elements accumulated in the universe over billions of years, and star systems with planets began to form.

To prove that this did happen in our past the secular science community is pointing its finger to a huge horn that was built. They pointed the horn out into space and they heard static. Scientists are saying that this static is radiation left over from the big bang. Why can't this static be just radiation left over from an exploding sun or solar flare? How can they say that this radiation is coming from an ancient explosion? They have no proof that the radiation they hear is actually from the big bang. It is a theory that the science community is saying is fact. Not real proof, just a theory.

Another problem with the Big Bang theory is. Where did the gas and matter come from to begin with? You cannot form gas, energy, and matter; they do not appear from nothing. That is why the Big Bang does not explain the beginning of the universe.

Dr. Hubble is a brilliant mathematician and astrologer who discovered that the universe is expanding away from each other. He came up with the mathematical formulas to calculate this expansion. Scientists are saying that this expansion is caused by the explosion of the big bang. However, if everything is floating away from everything else then how was anything formed? There is no evidence, mathematical or otherwise, that things slowed down. How did anything clump together to be formed if it is all drifting apart? In fact, astronomers are seeing things pulled apart instead of clumping together.

Originally the big bang theory was that there was a dense piece of matter that exploded. When you try to put the universe back into its beginning origin point, mathematically, it will not converge as a whole object. That is when they came up with this cloud theory. They are still having trouble making THIS theory work. The world is accepting this theory to be correct when the secular scientist cannot get it to work.

Scientists like Albert Einstein want us to believe that our Sun was created first. One uniformitarian belief presented in the textbooks is the formation of elements that make up the universe. The textbooks suggest that all of the matter in the universe is a result of the big bang. Atoms larger than hydrogen (with the exception of some helium and trace amounts of lithium which also formed from the energy of the big bang) are believed to be formed in the core of stars as a result of nuclear fusion. This process can only explain the presence of elements up to the mass of iron. It is suggested that the elements heavier than iron formed as a result of supernovae exploding. These elements were scattered into the universe and were eventually gathered by forming stars and planets.

The formation of a protostar over millions of years from a spinning nebula has been proposed to explain the birth of new stars. There are many problems with this scenario and no explanation of how the first stars could have formed according to the known laws of physics. The Bible explains that God made the stars on day four. According to secular science the heavier elements found on the earth were produced in a supernova and were collected as the solar system formed.

This stands in direct opposition to the creation of the earth described in Genesis. The Bible presents the view that God created the entire universe, including each individual atom, out of nothing in six days, not from the constant process of stellar evolution over billions of years. The Bible teaches that the earth was formed on Day One and the stars on Day Four through the spoken words of God—the two ideas are quite opposite.

Everything in our solar system was created for **our** benefit. Mercury was created to show us what will happen to objects that are too close to the Sun. Venus, once considered our sister planet. Venus is there to show us what would happen to the gas planets if they were closer to the Sun. Mars is to show us what our planet would look like without the protective layer of our atmosphere. Jupiter serves many functions. Jupiter is our protector by using its gravity and shooting harmful asteroids and comets out into outer space away from us. It also shows us what a gas planet looks and acts like with a large amount of gravity. Also, how Jupiter's many moons affect the surface of Jupiter, which in turn shows us what would happen to the surface of the Earth if we had multiple moons. Saturn shows us the beauty of its rings and how it affects its surroundings. Uranus shows us what a planet on its side looks like. Neptune shows us what a frozen gas planet looks like. Pluto and the other dwarf planets show us what the outer universe, so far away from the heat of the Sun, looks like. Each planet has something to teach us.

The more scientists look at other solar systems the more unique our solar system seems to be. In the past two decades, astronomers have discovered hundreds of planets orbiting other stars. They are large Jupiter-sized planets orbiting very close to their star—the opposite of what was predicted by secular models. With the secular models the astronomers expected to find other Earths in the "Goldilocks" zone. The Astronomers are not finding this to be true. They are not PERFECT worlds like ours seems to be.

Hand Out #2
Space and Time

A new theory is arising from Christian astronomers. God is the one who created time. God works outside of our time line. Space and Time Theorems states, "Any universe that expands on average has a spacetime beginning, implying a Causal Agent outside space and time who creates space, time, matter, and energy. **Borde, Vilenkin, Guth.** The three secular scientists who wrote this just proved that God created space, time, matter, and energy. However, you notice that they do not want to admit it.

According to the dictionary, time is defined as this.

Time (tīm)*n.*

1.

a. A nonspatial continuum in which events occur in apparently irreversible succession from the past through the present to the future.

b. An interval separating two points on this continuum; a duration: *a long time since the last war; passed the time reading.*

c. A number, as of years, days, or minutes, representing such an interval: *ran the course in a time just under four minutes.*

d. A similar number representing a specific point on this continuum, reckoned in hours and minutes: *checked her watch and recorded the time, 6:17 am.*

e. A system by which such intervals are measured or such numbers are reckoned: *solar time.*

The reason I am emphasizing 1e is because time is a measurement. We use that measurement to tell us many things. The minute, hour, day, month, and year. God does not need time as a measurement. He is infinite no matter what. God is capable of doing everything that is written in Genesis 1:1-11 in 7 days because he is not limited to our measurement of time. One day to God could be one day, ten years, or even one thousand years.

We have to take God at his Word. When God says that He created everything in 7 days He means it. God does not lie. If we cannot believe God in that He is capable of creating in 7 days. Then we cannot believe him in any other parts of the Word of God, the Bible.

The beginning is not only found in Genesis 1:1 but is found elsewhere in the bible here are some more scriptures. Genesis 2:3-4, Psalms 148:5, Isaiah 40:26, 42:5, 45:18, John 1:3, Colossians 1:15-17, and Hebrews 11:3. If we read these passages, we see the big picture of creation. I do encourage you to read these passages.

Hand Out #
3 The God Particle

CERN was built in Switzerland for scientists to discover what they call "The God Particle". This is from Cern's home website.

The Brout-Englert-Higgs mechanism

In the 1970s, physicists realized that there are very close ties between two of the four fundamental forces – the weak force and the electromagnetic force. The two forces can be described within the same theory, which forms the basis of the <u>Standard Model.</u> This "unification" implies that electricity, magnetism, light and some types of radioactivity are all manifestations of a single underlying force known as the electroweak force.

The basic equations of the unified theory correctly describe the electroweak force and its associated force-carrying particles, namely the photon, and the W and Z bosons, except for a major glitch. All of these particles emerge without a mass. While this is true for the photon, we know that the W and Z have mass, nearly 100 times that of a proton. Fortunately, theorists Robert Brout, François Englert and Peter Higgs made a proposal that was to solve this problem. What we now call the Brout-Englert-Higgs mechanism gives a mass to the W and Z when they interact with an invisible field, now called the "Higgs field", which pervades the universe.

At CERN on 4 July, the ATLAS and CMS collaborations present evidence in the LHC data for a particle consistent with a Higgs boson, the particle linked to the mechanism proposed in the 1960s to give mass to the W, Z and other particles. (Image: Maximilien Brice/Laurent Egli/CERN)

Just after the big bang, the Higgs field was zero, but as the universe cooled and the temperature fell below a critical value, the field grew spontaneously so that any particle interacting with it acquired a mass. The more a particle interacts with this field, the heavier it is. Particles like the photon that do not interact with it are left with no mass at all. Like all fundamental fields, the Higgs field has an associated particle – the Higgs boson. The Higgs boson is the visible manifestation of the Higgs field, rather like a wave at the surface of the sea.

Candidate Higgs boson events from collisions between protons in the LHC. The top event in the CMS experiment shows a decay into two photons (dashed yellow lines and green towers). The lower event in the ATLAS experiment shows a decay into four muons (red tracks) (Image: CMS/ATLAS/CERN)

A problem for many years has been that no experiment has observed the Higgs boson to confirm the theory. On 4 July 2012, the ATLAS and CMS experiments at CERN's Large Hadron Collider announced they had each observed a new particle in the mass region around 125 GeV. This particle is consistent with the Higgs boson but it will take further work to determine whether or not it is the Higgs boson predicted by the Standard Model. The Higgs boson, as proposed within the Standard Model, is the simplest manifestation of the Brout-Englert-Higgs mechanism. Other types of Higgs bosons are predicted by other theories that go beyond the Standard Model.

On 8 October 2013 the Nobel prize in physics was awarded jointly to François Englert and Peter Higgs "for the theoretical discovery of a mechanism that contributes to our understanding of the origin of mass of subatomic particles, and which recently was confirmed through the discovery of the predicted fundamental particle, by the ATLAS and CMS experiments at CERN's Large Hadron Collider".

Allow me to try and summarize this information. The scientist at Cern built an underground magnet. The largest that the world has seen. In order to smash proton particles together in order to find the element that holds all objects together. They have done the smashing and so far, have not found this "God particle." They will not be able to find it because God is the glue that sticks everything together, not a particle.

I believe that all the scientist at Cern have missed the point of particle science. If we could see the world in its' entirety at the particle level, we would see that light is the most abundant element. If a person had the ability to control light particles, they would have the ability to destroy things at the smallest level. Light particles can pierce through solid objects. Electrons can create a glow of light. What do we know about God? We know that God is light. He can pierce through anything and He can keep us held together with the use of light.

Hand Out #4
What are Aliens?

Here are some Bible verses to help us answer this question.

Ezekiel 28:12-26

12 Son of man, take up a lamentation upon the king of Tyrus, and say unto him, Thus saith the Lord GOD; Thou sealest up the sum, full of wisdom, and perfect in beauty.

13 Thou hast been in Eden the garden of God; every precious stone was thy covering, the sardius, topaz, and the diamond, the beryl, the onyx, and the jasper, the sapphire, the emerald, and the carbuncle, and gold: the workmanship of thy tabrets and of thy pipes was prepared in thee in the day that thou wast created.

14 Thou art the anointed cherub that covereth; and I have set thee so: thou wast upon the holy mountain of God; thou hast walked up and down in the midst of the stones of fire.

15 Thou wast perfect in thy ways from the day that thou wast created, till iniquity was found in thee.

16 By the multitude of thy merchandise they have filled the midst of thee with violence, and thou hast sinned: therefore I will cast thee as profane out of the mountain of God: and I will destroy thee, O covering cherub, from the midst of the stones of fire.

17 Thine heart was lifted up because of thy beauty, thou hast corrupted thy wisdom by reason of thy brightness: I will cast thee to the ground, I will lay thee before kings, that they may behold thee.

18 Thou hast defiled thy sanctuaries by the multitude of thine iniquities, by the iniquity of thy traffick; therefore will I bring forth a fire from the midst of thee, it shall devour thee, and I will bring thee to ashes upon the earth in the sight of all them that behold thee.

19 All they that know thee among the people shall be astonished at thee: thou shalt be a terror, and never shalt thou be any more*.

20 Again the word of the LORD came unto me, saying,

21 Son of man, set thy face against Zidon, and prophesy against it,

22 And say, Thus saith the Lord GOD; Behold, I am against thee, O Zidon; and I will be glorified in the midst of thee: and they shall know that I am the LORD, when I shall have executed judgments in her, and shall be sanctified in her.

23 For I will send into her pestilence, and blood into her streets; and the wounded shall be judged in the midst of her by the sword upon her on every side; and they shall know that I am the LORD.

24 And there shall be no more a pricking brier unto the house of Israel, nor any grieving thorn of all that are round about them, that despised them; and they shall know that I am the Lord GOD.

25 Thus saith the Lord GOD; When I shall have gathered the house of Israel from the people among whom they are scattered, and shall be sanctified in them in the sight of the heathen, then shall they dwell in their land that I have given to my servant Jacob.

26 And they shall dwell safely therein, and shall build houses, and plant vineyards; yea, they shall dwell with confidence, when I have executed judgments upon all those that despise them round about them; and they shall know that I am the LORD their God.

Ezekiel gives us the story of Lucifer the Archangel. We see in this passage what happens to him and ⅓ of the angels that were kicked out of heaven with him. These angels are called the Fallen Angels, demons, Satan, and the Devil. The Bible also calls them many more names in Ephesians 6:12 For our struggle is not against flesh and blood, but against the rulers, against the authorities, against the powers of this dark world and against the spiritual forces of evil in the heavenly realms.

Revelation 12:7-9

7 Then war broke out in heaven. Michael and his angels fought against the dragon, and the dragon and his angels fought back.

8 But he was not strong enough, and they lost their place in heaven.

9 The great dragon was hurled down—that ancient serpent called the devil, or Satan, who leads the whole world astray. He was hurled to the earth, and his angels with him.

When the Fallen Angels were thrown out of Heaven they were thrown through the different layers of Heaven onto and into the layers of Earth. "So above is so below." According to the Bible there are a total of 10 different levels or dimensions to our known space.

Spiritual- this is where the Angels and demonic forces can coincide with us but we can not see them.

2D the flat plane- length and width

3D the filled plane- length, width, and depth

Time

Ozone layer- From the ground to Inner Space

Outer Space- Inner Space to the Throne of God

Heavenly- Throne of God

Abraham's Bosom- Luke 16:22-23 realm of the righteous souls before Jesus

Hades or Hell- Realm of Damnation

Tartarus- Deepest part of the Earth

The Earth also has three layers to it. The first layer going downwards is called Abraham's Bosom in Luke 16:22-23. This is where the righteous spirits stayed after they died and before Jesus released them after preparing a place in Heaven for them. The second layer is Hell or Hades. That is where the souls of the unrighteous go. The third layer is called Tartarus that is where Satan and all the Fallen Angels will be chained for 1,000 years. God did not put the Fallen Angels into just one area when He kicked them out of Heaven. They have the capabilities to do what all Angels of God can do. They can exist in any layer from the Depths of the Earth to the edge of Heaven. We can even see that Satan himself can still enter into certain parts of Heaven in the Book of Job. Job 1:6 Now there was a day when the sons of God came to present themselves before the LORD, and Satan came also among them.

Isaiah 14:12-15

12 How you have fallen from heaven, morning star, son of the dawn! You have been cast down to the earth, you who once laid low the nations!

13 You said in your heart, "I will ascend to the heavens; I will raise my throne above the stars of God; I will sit enthroned on the mount of assembly, on the utmost heights of Mount Zaphon.

14 I will ascend above the tops of the clouds; I will make myself like the Most High."

15 But you are brought down to the realm of the dead, to the depths of the pit.

Job 1:7

And the LORD said unto Satan, Whence comest thou? Then Satan answered the LORD, and said, From going to and fro in the earth, and from walking up and down in it.

We see from this passage that Satan is not yet in the depths of the pit. He is still able to roam the Earth.

2 Corinthians 4:4

The god of this age has blinded the minds of unbelievers, so that they cannot see the light of the gospel that displays the glory of Christ, who is the image of God.

John 8:44

You belong to your father, the devil, and you want to carry out your father's desires. He was a murderer from the beginning, not holding to the truth, for there is no truth in him. When he lies, he speaks his native language, for he is a liar and the father of lies.

The Fallen Angels have dominion in outer space. We have dominion on Earth. The Fallen Angels became evil and demonic no longer angelic.

Genesis 6:2

That the sons of God saw the daughters of men that they were fair; and they took them wives of all which they chose.

Genesis 6:4

There were giants in the earth in those days; and also after that, when the sons of God came in unto the daughters of men, and they bare children to them, the same became mighty men which were of old, men of renown.

Genesis 6:5

And GOD saw that the wickedness of man was great in the earth, and that every imagination of the thoughts of his heart was only evil continually.

The Fallen Angels are able to create children with human females. The hybrid created giants in the Old Testament. The current demonic angels "aliens" are creating hybrid children today if you believe survivors' testimonies. However, the new hybrids are genetically altered so they look more like us. One of the reasons for this might be that they will use these hybrid children to help deceive us in some way. One way is to help us think wickedly continually instead of God and heavenly things.

Most present day tv, movies, and music is sinful in nature. Demonic forces use these to help us think wickedly at all times. Our technologies help to spread evil across the globe. We have seen a decline in Church attendance as a result.

What are Aliens? Aliens are demonic entities who want us to worship them instead of God. They do whatever they can to deceive us into believing that they are gods. They do not want us to worship the true God, the creator of all things.

Hand Out #5
Genesis 1:16 The bible calls the Sun and Moon what?

The tribe of Israel is associated with the Moon. The Sun was called the Greater Light and the Moon was called the lesser light. God Created the Greater light to rule by day and the lesser light to rule by night. The word Sun does not appear until Genesis 15:12. Moon does not appear until Genesis 37:9. Humans called the Sun and Moon greater and lesser light till that point.

Joseph has a dream in Genesis 37 about the Sun, Moon, and Stars

- Sun- the father

- Moon- the mother

- Stars- the other 11 Constellations bow down before Joseph.

The Sun represents God the Father. The Moon represents the "Mother Land," or the Nation of Israel. The stars represent the sons of Israel or the twelve tribes. God puts in the Cosmic lights the entire tribe of Israel and Israel's history.

The different tribes have an emblem that is similar to a heavenly constellation.

- Example: Judah- a lion- Constellation, Leo.

The Heavens tell a story about Israel and the Messiah. The Year begins in the Virgin and the Year ends in the Lion. The story of the Messiah begins with the Virgin birth and ends with Him being the Lion of the tribe of Judah.

- Sign- A signal, a tolkien, or an omen.

- Season- A fixed time, An appointed time, and a Festival.

- Day-24 hours, 12 hours to 12 hours- sunset to sunrise, sunrise to sunset

- Year- an entire revolution of time.

Hand Out #6
God's Cosmic Time

- Earth- determines the day

- Moon- determines the month cycle- 29.5 days complete a lunar cycle from New Moon to New Moon.

- Sun- determines the Year- 365.25 days to complete a year- a solar year

- Stars- determines the seasons. Men have always looked to the stars to determine upcoming events because Stars are for Signs and Seasons.

Man started worshipping the stars.

It was never God's intention for His creation (the sun, moon, and stars) to be worshiped over the Creator (God the Father).

There are 12 Constellations from the Virgin to the Lion. God Created them to be signs and for the seasons.

The reason why God had the Israels associated with the moon and not the Sun. The Moon is a reflection of the Sun. The Sun is the Greater light and the Moon is the Lesser light. Without the light from the Sun there can be no Light in the Moon. "You have to depend on my light to be able to shine. If I do not shine on you, darkness will come to your nation and your country," saith the Lord.

Pagan's chose to worship the Sun not the Moon. God did not want His people to be tempted to worship the Sun so He chose the moon to represent His people. Sun worship leads to Idolatry. You still see Sun worshipping today in many major religions. If you want to know which ones, I think you need to pray about it and let God reveal it to you.

Israel is a lesser nation like the Moon is the lesser light. "You will be the lesser nation but I will illuminate on you to lighten a darkened world," saith the Lord.

With my light, word, and Tora, I will give you the tools to light the world in the night. At night the moon gives us light.

"Just like the Moon goes through cycles I will also allow you to go through cycles of your spiritual and natural history.' You, meaning Israel, 'will go to walking in darkness to Following Me to go back to walking in darkness," saith the Lord God knew they would do it. And that is why He chose the Moon as their National symbol.

The Moon has a 30-day cycle that represents the 30 generations prophetically. Abraham who is the start; who is the Father of Israel. "New Moon." There are 15 generations from Abraham to Solomon. Where the temple was built and it was Israel's peak in history. "Full Moon." Solomon's Son Rehoboam becomes King and Israel starts to decline. You come to 15 generations later you come to complete spiritual darkness and captivity in the time of Daniel. "New Moon again." Israel went from nothing. Just one man who believed, to full, Solomon and his golden temple, to nothing again, slavery and captivity in Babylon. We will see signs in the Sun, Moon and Stars Jesus says.

Hand Out #7
Primordial Goo

Let us talk about primordial goo. According to the Theory of Evolution everything began in primordial goo. There was an experiment that was conducted in 1953 by Stanley Miller. Miller was a graduate student of chemistry at the University of Chicago. Miller tried to demonstrate how life first emerged on Earth. Miller tried to reproduce the Earth's early atmosphere. He pumped hydrogen, methane, ammonia, and a small amount of water vapor into a maze of glassware then sparked the gasses with electrical discharges to simulate lightning. After five days, he discovered what he had hoped for. A few amino acids, the basic building blocks of living organisms, had collected in the dark residue at the bottom of the glass. Many said that this is proof that life could have formed in the oceans of the early Earth.

Since that experiment in the 1950s scientist theorized a different atmosphere of the early Earth. In the 1960s they changed the gasses of what would have been in the atmosphere which were carbon dioxide, nitrogen, and water vapor. When Miller redid his experiment using these gasses, he did not get amino acids. However, this experiment is still taught in classrooms today. Not as a failed experiment but as proof that life can start without God. Secular science keeps feeding everyone disinformation in order for their theories to work. I will show you that this is not the first time they do this.

Hand Out #8
Theory of Evolution

     Let us talk about the Theory of Evolution. In order for Evolution to work you have to have a lot of time. We have already discussed that the 4.5 billion years that is used to date the age of the Earth is flawed. The skeletons that are used to prove that man was once apes actually are just skeletons of ancient apes and show no evidence of these apes evolving into upright walking humanoids. A few of these skeletons become proof of the theory of Evolution later become debunked and not valuable.

     An example of this is the Piltdown Man. A skull was found in 1912 later called Piltdown Man. The New York Times picked up the story and wrote an article on December 22, 1912. The New York Times made the claim that the skull proved Darwin's Theory to be true. According to Sir Arthur Keith, it was the find of the 20th century. Sir Arthur Keith was the President of the Royal Anthropological Society of Great Britain. Sir Arthur Keith published a book in 1925 on the Piltdown Man. 500 articles were also written about the Piltdown Man. In 1953 someone went through the archives of the Society and discovered that the skull was a fake. They took the skull of a modern human, chemically altered it so it would appear older, replaced the lower jaw bone with an orangutan's jaw bone, and filed the teeth so it would fit perfectly. There are many more examples of how Evolutionists alter or cherry pick the evidence.

     An example of "cherry picking," is the DNA comparison of Apes and Humans. Even to this day we hear Evolutionists tell us that Humans and Apes are 98% compatible and this shows that we have "evolved" from them. I will try my best to break this down. In the human Genome (a full set of chromosomes; all the inheritable traits of an organism.) there are **3.097** billion base pairs. In an ape Genome there are **3.231** billion. That is an increase of 4.3% more chromosomes in apes than humans. Already you should be seeing a problem with this DNA comparison but I will go on to tell you how they came up with the 98%. To make the comparison the Genomes were so different that they had to break them down into chunks that were similar in order to even compare them. They excluded **25%** of human genetic material and **18%** of the chimps. In order for us to "evolve" from apes we would need 25% more DNA and they would need to lose 18% in order for us to even be close. Because of updates to technology a revised comparison has been done and we are now 66% to 86% compatible. That is a big difference to 98%. On the National Geographic website; it shows that humans are 88% similar to a mouse, 85% similar to a cow and 84% similar to a dog because we are all mammals.

The next problem with the theory of Evolution is there are no transitional fossils of creatures evolving from one animal into a different animal. In fact, the fossil record actually proves that all life starts at the same time period and not in stages like Charles Darwin's theory would suggest. The fossil record actually shows that one day there was no life at all. Then the next day all life is created it is called the Cambrian Explosion. Again, scientists prove that the Bible is correct.

Charles Darwin is most famous for his only proof that his theory was fact and that is Finches. In 1830, Darwin visited the Galapagos islands. He observed the finches that lived on the different islands. He found that the size and shape of their beaks tended to vary island by island. This was his proof that his theory was correct. He explained that nature selected the fittest birds to survive because certain types of beaks were better suited for gathering the food resources available on the different islands. Modern science has shown that Darwin's Finches are not evidence for Evolution. Modern studies have tracked over a thousand finches that lived in either rural or urban environments, to determine how and why their beak sizes and shapes would differ based on where they lived. The studies revealed significant differences in beak depth and width between urban and rural populations. The differences were caused by epigenetic mechanisms such as DNA methylation. Methyl tags changed the way a gene is expressed without changing its DNA. This mechanism enables rapid adaptation in finch beaks and other traits to enable them to fit into their environments. Even between just a couple of generations. So, rather than Darwin's evolutionary ideas explaining the changes. The finches show that God designed it that way.

This mechanism also explains how the human race can adapt to their environment and change their pigmentation and body types. Again, I will state there is only one race, the human race.

Hand Out #9
How did the Sabbath get moved from Saturday to Sunday?

That would be the Roman pagan influence. When Roman Emperor Constatine became a Christian in 331A.D. During the battle of Milan; Constatine says that he saw a sign in the sky of a cross. There was a banner going across the cross saying, "If you lead with this sign you will win." Constantine had his soldiers put a cross on their shields before they went to battle. Constantine won the battle; then became the Roman Emperor. Emperor Constatine wrote an edict that gave freedom to the Christians. Eventually Christianity became the religion for the entire empire of Rome. That is the good part of Constantine's conversion.

The bad part is that Emperor Constatine merges pagan practices with the Christian beliefs. He moved Sabbath from Saturday to Sunday. Sunday is the day of the Sun. Where the pagans worshiped the Sun. As I said before, Sun worship leads to idolatry. The Catholic Church still worships the Sun today. How can I say this? You will see crosses with rays of the sun coming out behind them. That is the merging of pagan and Christian icons together. They changed pagan temples into churches. They had priests lead the worship. It was priests who led worship in the pagan temples and not the Levite Priests of the Israelites. They burned incense to God instead to pagan gods. The Catholic Church still worshipped idols.

The Catholic church will say that Peter was the first Pope. However, Peter is not the one who started the Catholic church. The first Pope would be Emperor Constatine. It was Paul who was the first Apostle to go to Rome and started a church there. However, the church Paul started and the Catholic Church are not the same. Peter was Crucified upside down in the City of Rome. The mother of Emperor Constatine, Helen, did steal Peter's body along with other religious relics. Peter's body still resides in the catacombs under the Vatican to this day. Peter nor Paul had anything to do with the founding of the Catholic Church.

It is said that more Christians have been killed since Emperor Constantine's conversion than before he found God. When the Catholic Church was founded then they became the only Christian Church allowed to exist. They killed those who opposed it. This is another example of how the Catholic Church is not a Christian Church.

Hand Out #10
Map of Eden

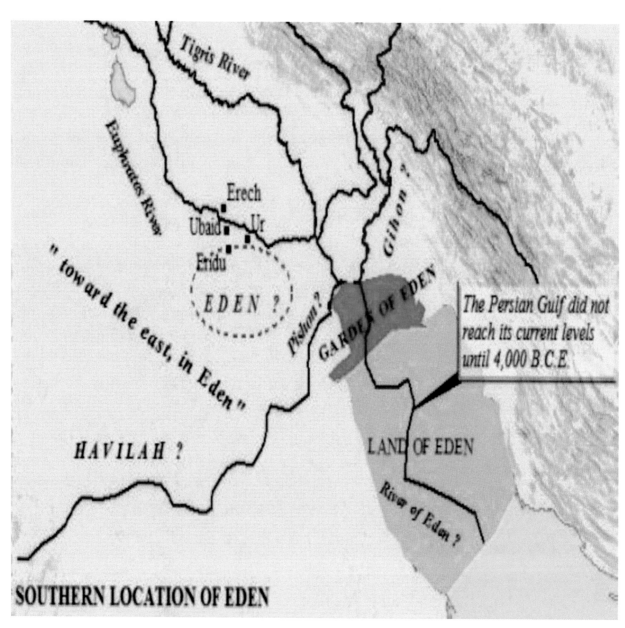

https://www.israel-a-history-of.com/old-testament-map.html#gallery[pageGallery]/1/

Hand Out #11
Genesis 3:21

For Adam also and for his wife the Lord God made coats of skins, and clothed.

This was the first animal sacrifice. This was the first time something had died on the whole planet. God showed Adam and Eve how He wanted animal sacrifice.

From the story of Cain and Abel we see another animal sacrifice. Cain offers grain to God but God does not accept this. Abel offers a lamb as offering and God is well pleased. Why did God not take the offering from Cain? Because the ground in which the food was grown from is cursed from Adam and Eve's original sin (Genesis 3:17). The lamb was a blood sacrifice to cleans Abel from this sin.

Why is there a blood requirement? The "original sin" cut humankind off physically from God. So, a physical action is required to gain access to God. Blood is what keeps us alive. Without blood we would die. God does not require us to spill the blood of humans. God loves us too much for our blood to be spilled. All He asked was an animal's blood to be used instead.

Leviticus 17:11 For the life of the flesh [is] in the blood: and I have given it to you upon the altar to make an atonement for your souls: for it [is] the blood [that] maketh an atonement for the soul.

Jesus later becomes the lamb that is slain for the "original sin." Because animal blood cannot completely forgive you of that "original sin."

Hebrews 9:12-14 Neither by the blood of goats and calves, but by his own blood he entered once into the holy place, having obtained eternal redemption [for us].

Since God can no longer walk with his creation in the garden. God, the master planner, had to come up with a plan B. From that point God arranged it for Jesus to die for the "original sin" so we could walk with God again. God sent prophets to us throughout history; to tell us what to expect. Some of us still missed the Messiah coming.

Made in the USA
Middletown, DE
02 June 2023

31937355R00027